Africa

*Your insouciant beauty,
your primitive serenity,
call me back to you...*

AFRICAN SAFARI

el babuino

BABOON

The sweetest sight I ever saw
was a newborn baboon with his ma.

Mama strode without a care,
While baby clung to her belly hair.

They trotted along the African plain,
Racing home as the sun began to wane.

He'll soon be able to hang on her back,
As she ambles along the dusty track.

el búfalo del Cabo
CAPE BUFFALO

Hello, hello Missus Cape Buffalo
You lumber along so heavy and slow...
Could it be you have no place to go?

But when provoked you can pick up the pace,
At thirty-five miles per hour you race.
With curly black horns draped about your face.

You are quite social, not really a nerd;
Rarely alone, you are part of a herd,
And your pal the cattle egret is your favorite bird.

While some people think that you look sorta weird,
By most folks you are positively revered,
For in all of Africa, you're among the most feared.

el guepardo
CHEETAH

Among all the cats he thinks he's the best,
He can easily outpace the rest.
Not one can surpass the cheetah's power
To sprint at 70 miles per hour.

He clocks zero to 60 in three seconds flat.
No other land animal can equal that!
He preys upon impala and the Thompson's gazelle,
And dines upon antelope and warthogs as well.

But when hunting in a group we call a coalition,
He seems to develop much more ambition.
He'll take down a zebra, ostrich or wildebeest,
Then sit and devour it in one giant family feast.

Unlike most felines, cheetah hunts in the day,
And can turn in mid-air while chasing his prey.
His long agile tail serves as a rudder,
To easily steer him from one direction to another.

Cheetahs don't roar when they're on the prowl,
But they can purr, chirp, hiss, meow and growl.
With long, strong legs and a lean torso,
He weighs a hundred fifty pounds or so.

Cheetah wears a coat that's tan and spotted.
He's such a handsome beast, I'm totally besotted.

el elefante
ELEPHANT

The elephant is like none other.
Sure, she has a father and mother,
But when it comes to size and shape,
The elephant truly takes the cake.

Elephant is a creature of contradiction
As if her maker couldn't make a decision.
Her tusks are long, smooth and pointy,
While her hide is wide and round and wrinkly.

She'll climb in the river to take a quick dunk,
And hose herself off with her thick agile trunk,
Then without a pause, she'll retreat to the shore,
To cover herself in mud once more.

She will carelessly trample down the brush,
And stomp on the plants without a blush,
But don't think that she's insensitive
Elephants are known to be very contemplative.

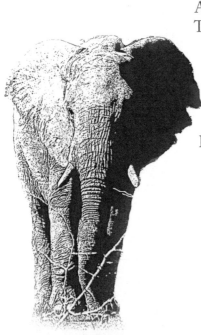

la jirafa
GIRAFFE

A salute to the giraffe

I love the giraffe,
I've loved him since he was a calf.
He's tall and svelte,
and lopes the veldt
At 35 miles per hour and a half.

He makes me laugh,
That handsome giraffe.
I like his dappled hide,
and his bulging thighs,
And the many curious features he hath.

His smart little head is adorned
With tiny round fur covered horns,
And two dainty pert ears,
That perk when danger nears,
To warn him it's time to adjourn.

I especially idolize,
His big, lovely, solemn, brown eyes.
Fringed with long lashes,
That blink when he dashes,
And make him seem terribly wise.

He sets up a mighty gale
With his scrawny brush tipped tail,
Which decorates his rear,
And the flies it does clear,
Till across the savanna they sail.

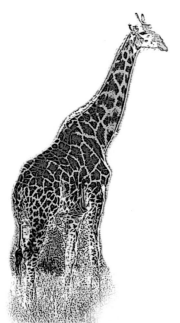

I'm so glad the giraffe was born,
Without him the world would be forlorn.
Oh, what the heck,
I'll mention his neck...
Above the treetops it's soarin'.

el hipopótamo

HIPPOPOTAMUS

The hippopotamus is fat and round.
His belly nearly touches the ground.
His legs are short and thick as trees,
I'm not even sure he has room for knees!

Hippo is a placid looking mammal,
He even seems a little bit bashful;
But don't be fooled by his docile demeanor...
It's hard to find an animal that's meaner.

el impala

IMPALA

I wonder what
the impala thought
as he bounced
across the clear blue sky.
Leap and land, jump and bounce,
Across the azure sky

I wonder what
the impala felt
As he soared over the African veldt
He looked like he was having such fun
under the gaze of the noon day sun...
I think I'd like to try.

el león
LION

Lion lazes under the sun
And sleeps the day away,
Until she spots the evening's glow
And knows it's time to prey.

She stealthily hides and scans the plains
As she crouches on a rock to spy.
Her pride will join her in the quest
For a hippo or zebra passing by.

When times are tough and food is scarce
The lion doesn't carry on.
It seems she's really not too proud
To feed her cubs on carrion.

el lagarto
LIZARD

Blue-headed agama lizard

He's only a lowly reptile
But still he likes to be in style,
So when he is in the proper mood
He can turn his skin from red to blue.
And if an insect wanders past,
His tongue will snatch it mighty fast.

el pingüino
PENGUIN

Excuse me if I like to gloat
About my shiny tuxedo-like coat

(It's really made of black and white feathers
And keeps me warm in all types of weathers.)

Or about how long I can swim in the sea
And make the little fish wary of me.

I'm proud to say that I'm faithful to my mate
And that we both help our eggs to incubate.

I know it's not really polite to boast
but could you survive on Africa's southern coast?

el rinoceronte

RHINOCEROS

Rhinoceros is a funny name
For an animal that's not so tame.
He has no front teeth in his massive pink gums,
And his big flat feet won't accommodate thumbs.

Rhino weighs a ton
and just for fun
He'll charge and make an awful stink
for any reason you can think.

Rhino is a true contrarian;
Also a staunch vegetarian.
Two horns protrude from his huge gray face;
Both seem comically out of place.

One in front and one behind,
Though it seems like Rhino doesn't mind.
But you will notice, there's no doubt,
The poor rhino is cursed with a homely snout!

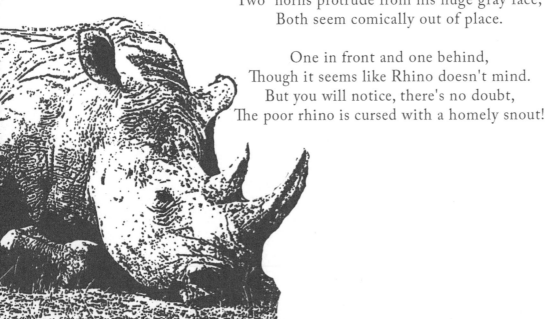

la amarillo-bill cigüeña
YELLOW-BILLED STORK

Who'd have thought that a beak,
So long and narrow and sleek,
Could sing out delish!
And snatch up a fish?
That yellow billed stork is a sneak!

el pájaro de sol
SUNBIRD

The sunbird's song

Good evening Missus Sunbird,
You are so drab and brown;
While your mate is draped
In a sapphire cape
Like he's headed for a night on the town.

Tiny Missus Sunbird,
Does he make you want to groan?
He has your same shape,
But sports a flamboyant nape,
And a little black cap on his crown.

Photo by Cheryl Cresta Turner 2014

el buitre
VULTURE

The vulture is a homely beast,
upon dead critters he does feast.

To find his meals he often relies,
not on his nose, but upon his eyes.

The vulture's not a popular creature,
but he possesses one salient feature:

When predators leave a mess to tend,
upon the vulture you can depend.

el waterbuck

WATERBUCK

The Waterbuck's Lament

Why do they call me a waterbuck?
With my thick shaggy coat
I surely can't float.
I prefer to wade in the muck.

Aquatics aren't really my sport.
I'm short and husky
And smell somewhat musky,
And I'm not much inclined to cavort.

But a lake can be very concealing,
So when enemies prey
On the shore I don't stay...
That's when I find water appealing!

la cebra
ZEBRA

Elegant in black and white
Zebra sways from left to right,
With strips that go up and down
And wind all the way around.

And if he isn't extremely tall,
Or incredibly large or very small,
Or even surprisingly chubby or thin,
He is remarkable for the skin he's in.

la dedicación
DEDICATION

This book is dedicated to

my wonderful grandchildren who inspired this book,

and to the children at Horne Elementary School in Houston, Texas

and to my husband, Don Turner,

who encouraged me to publish it.

All poems and photos are original work of the author
with the exception of the photos of
the sunbird and the lizard, which were taken by
Cheryl Cresta Turner

Made in the USA
San Bernardino, CA
23 February 2016